Contents

4 These playshapes are made from a kind of plastic.

6 Crude oil is found deep under the ground.

8 Crude oil is treated and changed at an oil refinery.

10 The plastic granules are made.

12 The playshapes are planned and designed.

14 The mould is designed and made.

16 Masterbatch and natural granules arrive at the factory.

18 An injection moulding machine is prepared.

20 The ingredients are fed into the machine.

22 The pieces are cooled and pushed out of the mould.

24 The finished playshapes are sorted and packed.

26 How a plastic toy is made

28 Plastic and its many uses

30 Plastic and the environment

32 Word bank and index

These playshapes are made from a kind of plastic.

The story of the playshapes starts with a substance called crude oil, which is also called petroleum. Most kinds of plastic are made from chemicals taken from crude oil.

▼ These plastic playshapes are coloured pieces. They are used to learn about shapes by creating patterns and pictures.

◄ This crude oil is black and thick. Sometimes crude oil is runny and clear, but mostly it is like brown treacle.

These playshapes are made out of a plastic called polypropylene copolymer. Different plastics often have long names like this.

Why plastic?

Plastic is a popular material because objects can be made quickly and easily. It can be moulded to make different shapes such as bottles and pipes. It can be pressed and stretched to make flat sheets of plastic. It can be made into fibres that can be used to make clothes. Plastic can be hard and clear like glass, soft and thick like a sponge, or thin and flexible like paper.

The word plastic comes from the Greek word *plastikos*, which means something that can be shaped and moulded.

Plastics are a popular material for making toys because they can be brightly coloured, and they are tough and waterproof.

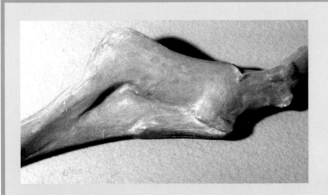

This prehistoric bone carving shows an early use of a natural 'plastic' material.

In the past

Early man discovered that materials such as bone and horn, and rubbery gum from tropical trees, were useful. Over time, people found that these materials could be shaped. Later, scientists discovered how to create synthetic plastics.

Crude oil is found deep under the ground.

Crude oil is trapped between layers of rock, deep under the ground. So oil rigs with powerful drills and other machinery are needed to reach it.

► Oil rigs can be found on land, or in the ocean.

The drill heads have to be very strong to drill through the rock, so they are usually made of strong steel and super-hard diamonds. A very long pipeline carries the crude oil back to the oil rig.

◄ Oil crews operate the huge machinery.

▲ Some oil tankers are so big that the crews use bicycles to travel from one end to the other.

What is crude oil?

Crude oil formed over millions of years, from the remains of plants and animals. It can be found in pockets under layers of rock. It is often very deep under the ground. Most crude oil is made into fuels that can be used for heating and transport. There is a limited amount of crude oil in the earth. One day it will run out.

Huge amounts of crude oil are pumped out of the ground each day. The oil is taken to oil refineries to be processed. Sometimes large tankers are used to transport it by sea.

Sometimes the oil is pumped along pipelines that are built across land.

▲ This pipeline is taking oil to a refinery.

Crude oil is treated and changed at an oil refinery.

Crude oil has to be changed before it is useful. At the oil refinery it is broken down into useful parts, such as fuels, gases and chemicals. The chemicals can be used to make plastics.

▲ Oil refineries have docks where the tankers unload the crude oil. They have pipelines, containers and machines to refine the crude oil.

To create plastics, the chemicals are heated and broken down into parts called monomers. This is called cracking. The monomers are the basic building blocks used to make different plastics. The different plastics can be made into a wide range of products such as tough car bumpers, soft plastic packaging and even fabrics to make clothes.

▲ This scientist is testing a liquid plastic to see how quickly it goes hard as it cools.

Plastics discovery

In 1951, two chemists called Hogan and Banks were trying to make a type of fuel. When their equipment got clogged up with a sticky, white substance they realised they had made an interesting discovery. As they had recorded what they had done so far they were able to recreate it. Their discoveries led to the manufacture of polypropylene.

Most crude oil is made into fuels such as petrol.

The plastic granules are made.

The playshapes are made from two types of plastic granule. One type of granule is called 'natural' because it is white and almost see-through. Natural granules are the main ingredient used to make playshapes.

▲ Natural granules look white.

▲ There are three types of masterbatch granules used to make the three colours of the playshapes - red, blue and yellow.

The other type of granule is called masterbatch. This is a special ingredient in plastic making. Just a tiny amount of masterbatch adds colour and other qualities to the finished plastic.

Both types of granules are made by a plastics factory.

To make the granules the plastic is heated to make it soft. Then it is pushed and squeezed through a machine to make long strands.

When the strands cool and go hard, they are chopped into small pieces called granules.

The makers of the playshapes order the granules they need from the plastics factory.

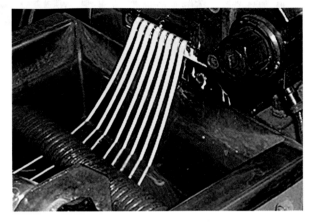
▲ The yellow masterbatch is squeezed into strands.

▲ The yellow masterbatch is now in granules.

They will mix the natural and masterbatch granules together, to make the correct colour plastic.

◀ The makers of the playshapes use samples to check the colour plastic the granules will make.

The playshapes are planned and designed.

Before anything can be made with the plastic granules, there is work to be done in the design department.

► Plans and designs are worked out using CAD, which means Computer Aided Design.

Ideas are discussed and sketched out first. Then every detail - colour, type of plastic, size and shape - can be tried and tested on a computer.

◄ Even a very simple plastic product needs to be planned and designed carefully.

Once a design is finalised, a prototype or a model is made. It might be made in different colours or with different plastics, to test them out and to find out what looks and works best.

Testing plastic toys

Toys have to be tested carefully to make sure they are safe to use. The manufacturer has to be sure the toy could not choke a child, that it is not toxic, or poisonous, and that it has no sharp edges.

Toys are also tested with children to make sure they are suitable.

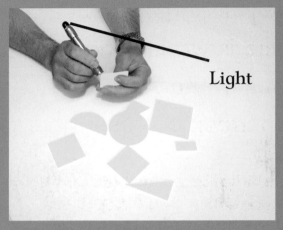

Light

▲ In the sharp test, a special tool that looks like a pen is touched on the plastic. If it lights up, the toy is too sharp.

► The plastics company test their products in a school to make sure they work properly.

▲ In the choke test, pieces are put in a small pot. If they fit in the pot, the pieces are too small.

The mould is designed and made.

A mould is designed for each toy. It is important that the mould is made very carefully. Once it is completed it will be used to make large quantities of an item, so the pieces the mould makes need to be perfect.

▲ Moulds are also designed using a computer.

◀ Plans for the mould are drawn up and checked.

Once the mould design is ready, computer-programmed machines make the mould. The mould for the playshapes is made out of a steel block. Steel is a metal which is very hard-wearing.

Drills   Steel block   Control panel

► The mould machine is controlled by a computer. The machine has drills to make the parts of the mould.

▲ The block of steel is very heavy!

Steel or aluminium?

Moulds are made of aluminium if it is a short run (10,000 pieces or less) or more hard-wearing steel for a long run. These playshapes have been made for a long time, over 30 years, so the mould is made from a steel block.

Masterbatch and natural granules arrive at the factory.

Plastic granules and masterbatch are bought in from different suppliers. The granules arrive in big bags.

► The bags of granules are packed in boxes and arrive on a lorry.

A supply of natural granules and bags of red, yellow and blue masterbatch are needed to create the playshapes. The materials are stored in a warehouse until they are needed.

◄ Bags of natural granules.

Now that everything is ready, the mould is taken to the machine that makes the plastic playshapes.

▲ The mould is very heavy so it is wheeled into the factory on a trolley.

Why plastic?

Plastic is a versatile, lightweight and tough material. It can be made into a wide range of different products from cling film that is light and flexible, to window frames that are hard and strong.

Many parts of cars are now made of plastic, because it can be light but very tough.

An injection moulding machine is prepared.

▼ The injection moulding machine has several parts.

Clamping unit
(the mould goes
inside here)

Worker waiting to
collect the shapes, which
come through a funnel

Computer

Injection
unit

Granule
feeder

An injection moulding machine is used to make
the playshapes. Injection moulding is especially
good for making many pieces at the same time.
The machine has three main parts: an injection
unit, a mould and a clamping unit.

First, the mould is fitted into the machine.

▲ The mould is lifted into the machine by a small crane.

The moulding machine is controlled by a computer.

▲ The machine's computer needs to be set, or 'told what to do', first. So information about the running time and temperature is typed in.

Moulding machines

There are different kinds of moulding machine. These machines use different ways to push the plastic into the mould. The injection moulding machine squirts the plastic into the mould. Other machines push, blow or squeeze the plastic to fill the mould to make the right shapes.

Bottles are made with a blow mould. Air is blown into the plastic to push it to the sides of a mould. This makes a hollow plastic shape.

The ingredients are fed into the machine.

The playshapes are made of 99% natural granules and 1% masterbatch granules.

► Only a tiny amount of masterbatch is needed.

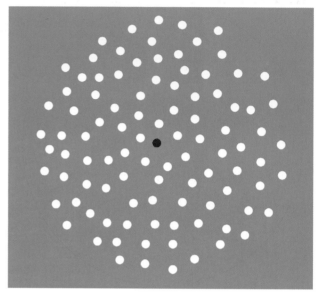

The natural granules are stored in a container called a hopper. The hopper is linked to the injection moulding machine by a pipe that runs across the factory's ceiling.

Pipe

Granules

Hopper

◄ A good supply of natural granules is kept in a hopper.

The masterbatch is fed directly into the machine. The first shapes to be made are the yellow ones. So yellow-coloured masterbatch is used.

► The two sorts of granules are in feeders in the machine.

Natural granules   Yellow masterbatch

rim

The natural and masterbatch granules are heated to 200°C. The mixture becomes molten, which means a very hot liquid. It goes into a canal system and is forced into the mould. More pressure is applied to make sure that the mould is completely filled with plastic.

◄ The mould produces 62 shapes at once. The machine makes them in 58 seconds. The pieces are attached to a rim.

The pieces are cooled and pushed out of the mould.

When the pieces are cool, the mould is opened and the pieces are pushed out. The playshapes fall down into a funnel. They are put into bags by hand. Each bag is weighed to make sure all 62 pieces are there.

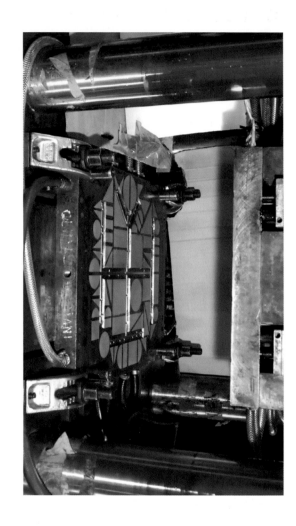

▶ The two sides of the mould open and the finished pieces are pushed out.

◀ A funnel makes it easier to catch the shapes in a bag.

The discarded rim is put in a box. The rims will be ground up and reused as plastic granules.

▶ The discarded rims are called sprue.

The machine will make hundreds of batches of the 62 yellow pieces. When the machine has made enough yellow pieces it is heated to a very high temperature to clean it. A different masterbatch is added and the next colour pieces are made. The machine makes the same number of playshapes in blue and then red.

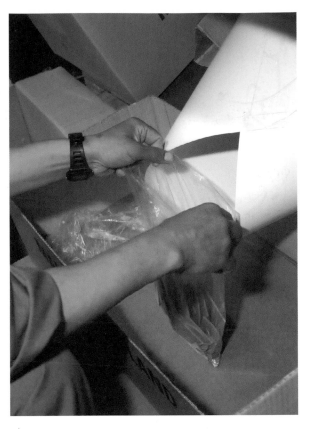

▲ The machine makes a batch of blue shapes next.

Plastic symbols

There are many types of plastic and each one is made with a different mixture of chemicals. Before plastics can be recycled they need to be sorted into types. These symbols show what type of plastic an object is made from.

This is the symbol for polypropylene.

▲ The red shapes are made to complete the set. Here they are being weighed.

The finished playshapes are sorted and packed.

▲ The playshapes are put into bags that are made of plastic too.

In the packing room, a bag of each playshape colour is put into a larger bag.

Large boxes are filled with batches of playshapes. Then they are sealed and labelled, and stored in the warehouse.

◀ The boxes are packed carefully so that they can be transported safely.

The plastic playshapes are ready to be
sent out to shops and schools to be used
to create patterns and pictures.

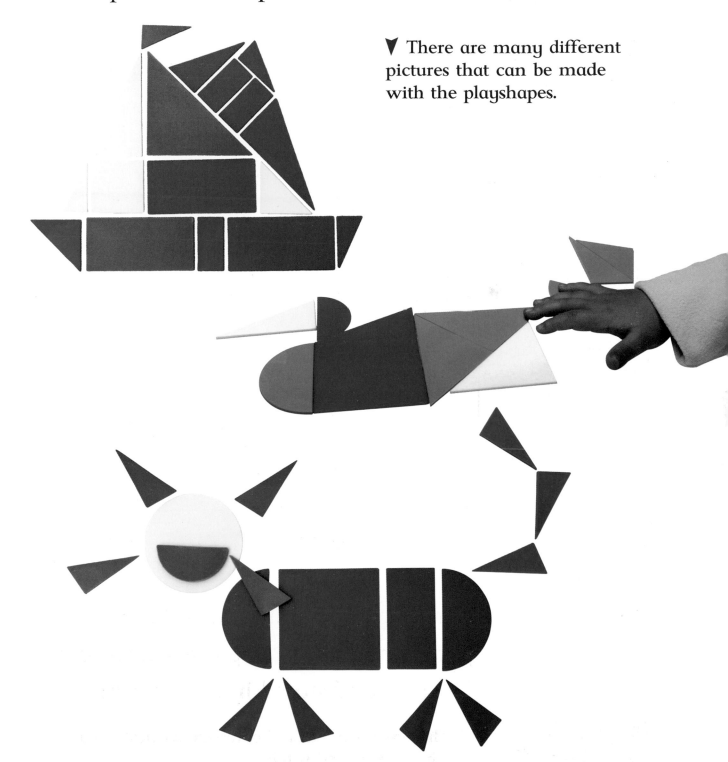

▼ There are many different
pictures that can be made
with the playshapes.

How a plastic toy is made

1. Most plastics are made from crude oil.

4. Chemicals taken from crude oil are used to make plastic granules.

2. Crude oil is drilled from the ground.

5. The playshapes, and their mould, are planned and designed.

3. At the refinery the crude oil is processed.

6. The mould is fitted into the machine.

7. Natural granules are fed into the machine.

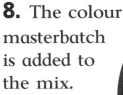

8. The colour masterbatch is added to the mix.

9. The hot plastic cools in the mould.

10. The finished pieces are pushed out and caught in a bag.

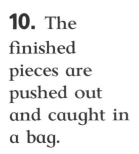

11. The playshapes are sorted and put into bags.

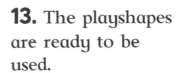

12. Boxes are filled and taped up ready for shipping.

13. The playshapes are ready to be used.

Plastic and its many uses

Plastic is used to make a huge range of different products, from toys to car parts. It has replaced other packaging materials because plastic is sturdier than paper or cardboard, and it is tougher and much lighter than glass.

◄ Plastic bags are light but strong, so they are ideal for carrying shopping.

▲ Fruit and vegetables are put in plastic containers and covered with plastic film to keep them clean and to protect them from bumps and knocks.

▲ Polystyrene is a type of plastic material that is mixed with air to make it soft and light. It is often used for packaging.

◄ Before plastic was invented, combs were made of materials such as bone or wood.

This plastic bottle is ideal for drinks and it won't break if you drop it. Plastic lunchboxes are good for food because they keep it clean and dry.

This torch is made with tough plastic. The waterproof casing will keep the batteries and bulb dry.

These sunglasses are made from two different plastics, one for the frames and a specially made plastic to protect your eyes from the sun.

Fleece material is very warm.

Plastic bottle to fluffy fleece

Did you know that a certain type of plastic can be recycled to make fleece material? This is PET plastic (Polyethylene Terephthalate), which is often used to make bottles for soft drinks. First, the labels and bottle tops are removed. Then the bottles are chopped into plastic flakes. The flakes are heated to melt them, and the soft plastic is pushed through holes in a machine to make long strands. The strands are stretched and squeezed, and then fluffed and cooled. This makes fibres that can be woven into fleece material.

Plastic and the environment

While a lot of plastic products are made to be used again and again, most plastic packaging is made to be thrown away. The main problem with plastic waste is that it does not biodegrade, which means that it does not break down or rot.

Lightweight plastics

Plastics are ideal for packaging because they can be very lightweight.

▶ Plastic packaging protects food and keeps it clean and fresh, and so cuts down on food waste.

However, these lightweight plastics can easily be blown away.

◀ Plastic litter can be blown around, which looks unsightly. But it also gets caught in trees and hedges, and plastic bags can block drains and streams.

Plastic and wildlife

Plastic waste and litter can be dangerous for wildlife. Gulls search piles of rubbish looking for food, and plastic waste can be swallowed or get caught on their legs or heads. Sea turtles swallow and choke on plastic bags because they mistake them for jellyfish, their favourite food.

► A bird caught in a piece of plastic waste.

Before the plastics can be recycled by machines, they usually have to be sorted into the different types by hand.

Recycling plastics

Recycling plastics saves energy and water, and also cuts down on pollution, but it is difficult because each plastic is different. Each type of plastic needs to be recycled separately. And in order for it to be worth doing, we all need to send more plastic for recycling, and to buy more things made from recycled plastics.

Word bank

Chemical A substance made up of atoms. Atoms are the building blocks that make up different substances.

Design To plan and make something, by making drawings, choosing materials, and deciding on shapes, colours and patterns.

Fuel A substance burned to make heat or power.

Manufacturer Someone who makes a product, especially on a large-scale using machinery.

Mould A container that gives shape to plastics and other materials.

Process A series of actions that cause a change.

Prototype A model that is made to test materials, patterns and colours.

Recycle To process and treat a material so that it can be used to make something else.

Refine To separate a mixture into its different parts.

Renewable resource A raw material, such as wood from trees, that can be replaced. Resources such as oil, gas and metals that have taken millions of years to form, cannot be replaced.

Synthetic A material made in a factory using chemicals.

Temperature A measure of heat.

Warehouse A building where things are stored.

Index

environmental issues 30-31

fuel 7, 8, 9

moulding machine 18, 19, 20

oil 4, 6, 7, 8, 9
oil refinery 7, 8

petroleum 4
plastic,
   history of 5, 9
   ingredients 4, 9
   granules 10, 11, 12, 16, 18, 20, 21, 22
   masterbatch 10, 11, 16, 20, 21, 23
   packaging 9, 28
   symbols 23

plastic (continued),
   uses of 5, 28, 29

recycling 23, 29 31

toy,
   design 12
   mould 14, 25, 28, 19, 21, 22
   testing 12, 13